MORE THAN ONE VOICE

CHANGING OUR WORLD STARTS WITH A GIRL

A collection of stories by  **Global Girl Project**

First Printed in United Kingdom, 2020

Published by Conscious Dreams Publishing
www.consciousdreamspublishing.com

Edited by Kate Nowakowski, Ruksana Hussain and Max Besana

Designed and typeset by Camila Gabrielle Frasson

Illustrated by Paloma Aravaca Sinnige

ISBN: 978-1-913674-22-9

"Never doubt that a small group of thoughtful, committed, citizens can change the world. Indeed, it is the only thing that ever has."

Margaret Mead

"To our global girls throughout the world who are conspiring, networking, inspiring, and mobilising groups of global social activists to change our world."

Julia Lynch,
Founding Director of Global Girl Project

MORE THAN ONE VOICE

CONTENTS

MORE THAN ONE VOICE

ACKNOWLEDGEMENTS

Our world continues to turn because of the connections we make with those who come into our network through shared ways of thinking, experiences, and connections. Global Girl, as an organisation, and by extension, this book, continues to turn on our global axis for the very same reason. We continue to be a bold life- and community-changing organisation because of the beautiful souls who come out of their networks to be a part of ours. All of our projects came to fruition, thanks to the determination and energy of our volunteers. This book is one of the best expressions of how to use your life to make a difference.

Without the following powerful women, this book would not be sitting in your hands right now, so join me in expressing gratitude to each of them for stepping up and stepping out. Thank you to Max Besana for teaching each of our authors how to truly tell a story, how to take what you are feeling on the inside and put it into words that can be felt by the reader. Gratitude to Paloma Aravaca Sinnige, whose attention to the minute details of each of our authors and their home communities translated into the colourful illustrations that help you feel as if you are sitting alongside our girls as they tell their stories. Without the discerning vision of our editorial ninjas, Kate Nowakowski and Ruksana Hussain, we would have never been able to walk that fine balance between your hearing the stories in the unique voice of each girl and making the book palatable for native English speakers. And then, of course, huge thanks to our design guru extraordinaire, Camila Gabrielle Frasson, who has been like the conductor of our orchestra, bringing all of the parts together into one beautiful and inspiring whole.

Our authors come from various countries around the world, and only one speaks English as her first language. Many of our girls live in remote villages with limited internet connectivity and no access to computers. To overcome these hurdles, we needed to rely on the kindness and connections of a number of global volunteers to get these stories to us, translate them, and reach back out to our girls when we had more questions! We want to send a huge amount of gratitude to Tashi Sherpa and Anu Ghising Tamang from Nepal for helping us contact our authors and translate their stories. Thank you to Martin Lahai from Sierra Leone who helped us be in contact with Aisata from his village, as she doesn't have a working phone, messaging apps, or a computer. And gratitude to Ifti Uddin who helped us translate Jiya's story from Urdu to English, to Max who helped translate Anny's story from Portuguese to English, and to Ludmille Lyvert who translated Ashleycka's story from Haitian Creole into English.

Lastly, thank you is really not enough of a sentiment to express what we feel about our eight young female authors. For each of you to trust Global Girl Project with your very personal stories and to share them in this powerful form, gratitude to every one of you. Thank you to each of you for being the impetus to our director, who thought up this magical idea in the first place. It is through your vulnerability and honesty that the idea was born.

INTRODUCTION

What would make you a good leader? How can you build a life that creates change? What do you want to do to change our world? These questions are at the base of the work we do at Global Girl Project, questions we want every young person to ask themselves and each other. These are also the questions our girls answer in their inspiring and very personal stories.

The tie that binds our eight authors together is their participation in the Global Girl Project Leadership Training & Cultural Exchange. Global Girl Project (GGP) was a milestone on the journey to leadership for each of our girls, the first time they travelled abroad and the first time they were able to share their dreams and ambitions with other girls from other cultures, yet it is just one piece of their stories.

Each of our authors has a different story of what it means to grow up as a girl in their countries and communities, from India to Haiti and Sierra Leone. Each of them has her own distinct voice, a voice being used to lead, create community change, and reach for what they most desire.

The following eight stories came to us in many languages—in Urdu, in Nepali—over Facebook Messenger in photos of handwritten pages. Sharing the stories of these remarkable young women was a process beset with challenges and far from conventional. One of our authors had to walk for two hours through the mountains of Nepal to reach the house of a friend with an internet connection and a warm fire. Another could only be reached after a volunteer in her village had gone to her home to share messages with her.

In the face of physical, technological, and cultural barriers, the stories of young women such as our authors often go untold. The potential of these stories to capture the imagination of a new generation of girls was motivation enough to ensure we rose to the challenge and saw the project through to fruition. When we rise up to surmount the challenges facing us, we discover where our true power lies and learn that there is always a way forward. The following eight stories tell us, in their own words and nuances, how to lead like a girl.

Julia Lynch,
Founding Director of Global Girl Project
www.globalgirlproject.org

मम्मी की तरह ताकतवर

Mighty Like Mummy

SHREE

- from India -

My father died when I was ten years old. He died in the morning, and that same day, in the evening, my mother brought a new man home and said, "He's your new father." I was very upset with my mother, but she thought that being a single mother meant she wouldn't be able to raise her three children.

For the next year, this new father beat my mom and me almost every day. I have two older brothers. They had the freedom to go out and take some time for themselves and escape the abusive situation, but my reality was very different. Even though I too needed mental and physical space to overcome the situation, I wasn't allowed to go out on my own. Where I am from, it is

believed that if you are a girl, you can't take care of yourself. Not being able to do anything alone or independently and being told that I couldn't take care of myself destroyed my confidence.

It's been eight years since I stopped living with my stepfather, but I still feel that I'm not stronger than a man. This is due to the things I was told and made to feel all my life.

I live in India's biggest city, Mumbai. Thanks to the NGO Kranti*, where I have lived for the last eight years, I learnt to know my rights and received an education. I have also been working with a therapist to overcome my childhood trauma, but still, I am struggling to believe in myself. There are many girls like me in India, and even around the world, who possess the capacity to change their life situation, but they are afraid.

They think, what if people don't agree with my decision to study, or my decision not to get married, or to cut my hair short? Will I get in trouble? What if I lose my life just because I speak up for my fundamental rights?

In my experience, most men don't display this fear of judgement, the fear of getting into trouble just because they have raised their voices. They do not fear losing their lives for these reasons.

I used to think that without a man, surviving and running a house was impossible. This is what I learnt from my mother. But was this really true?

> "What if I lose my life just because I speak up for my fundamental rights?"

---

*Kranti is a non-governmental organization (NGO) that empowers girls from Mumbai's red light areas to become agents of social change.

I was born and brought up in Mumbai, but my mother is from a village in southern India. In Mumbai, my stepfather was in charge of running the house, but when we used to visit our village, I could see my mother was the boss by the way she wore her confidence and took everything under her charge. It was in the village when she didn't have a man around, that I saw the strongest side of her as a woman. This made one thing very clear in my mind: people need to be given the opportunity to do something. Because my stepfather wasn't there, she took care of everything, and she was capable of achieving anything. It was society that made her feel as if she couldn't be equal to a man. It was society that didn't give her enough opportunities to do what she wanted.

"I got to comprehend what it is that makes a person a true leader."

My name is Shree, and I'm 19 years old. I live in an NGO called Kranti, which works with the daughters of sex-workers and girls who are born and brought up in Mumbai's red-light area. Kranti teaches us how to become agents of social change and how to be leaders in our own communities. Through Kranti, I have attended a two-month leadership programme in the United States, called Global Girl Project (GGP). In that project, I learnt many leadership skills and I got to comprehend what it is that makes a person a true leader. During that time, I learnt a lot about myself.

I have always been good at expressing myself through theatre, dance, communicating, and writing. If you want to be a leader, expressing yourself is important but also, it is important to be a good listener. I used to think that being able to communicate would be enough to be a leader, but in truth, there are so many other things that are necessary. I feel everyone has what it takes to be a leader, but it is up to each of us to bring out our own leadership skills. These are the things that I learnt at GGP, but learning alone wasn't enough. I wanted to use what I learnt in places where it was most needed. So, from October to December 2019, I was in Punjab, working with adolescent girls in the village of Bajwa Kalan, facilitating a play where the girls could voice the challenges facing them when achieving their dreams. The girls had written and directed scenes about early marriage, girls dropping out of school early, and caste discrimination. They performed this play at the village festival to raise awareness about these issues, surrounded by their whole community, through the medium of theatre. This journey was one of the best examples of my leadership. Not only was it important for me, but each one of these girls became a leader in their own communities.

We all face these kinds of problems in our neighbourhoods, communities, and countries, but what matters is that we take a stand for what is right. What matters is being leaders and creating leaders around us. I could see this happening in Punjab, and that is what success means to me.

Pou kisa an Ayiti

Why in Haiti

ASHLEYCKA
- from Haiti -

Hello everyone! My name is Ashleycka, and I am 19 years old. I am the third child in my family, and I have two big brothers. I also have two big sisters from my dad's side. I was born in Port-au-Prince, Haiti, and I live with my mother as I am her sole daughter. My favourite food is white rice and vegetables, and when I have time, I like to play games with kids and read. At the moment, I am in professional school, learning how to be a cook. I love to cook, and I know that I can earn some money working at a restaurant, but what I really want to be is a paediatrician. I'm going to work so hard as a cook, so I save up enough money to study and become a doctor.

Today, I want to speak in the name of all girls who live in Haiti but who are unlikely to be heard. The area I live in is especially neglected, and it does not feel as if anyone cares about us, something that bothers me a lot because some girls here grow up not trusting anyone. In Haiti, from the age of 13, it is challenging to avoid getting pregnant. When girls find themselves in this situation,

> "I want to speak in the name of all girls who live in Haiti but who are unlikely to be heard."

most parents don't want or are not able to support them. Usually, it is because they don't have the means. Most fathers don't assume responsibility and most moms don't have much money. They make small trades, but this does not bring back enough for them to pay the rent or eat. Other times, parents throw the girls out of the house. As a result of this, girls find themselves in the streets with nothing and no friends. No thanks to the Good Lord, but I have seen many cases of this. When a child is born on the street, I feel like it might become a bad child because they have no one to help them, no one to give them advice.

I think I am fortunate because I always had the support of my family, especially my mom and my two big brothers. They have supported me through many difficult times, like when I had to complete my secondary studies. To do so, you must first pass an exam. When the day came, I was very anxious, and I cried a lot, but they helped me and comforted me, and in the end, they had my back, and that aided me in passing my exams.

I also had the support of Foundation TOYA*, an organisation that works with girls. A friend of mine invited me to join them. Girls need a place to discover their capacity and their value; this is what we learnt at Foundation TOYA. There, I had the opportunity to learn how to make great choices. I joined Foundation TOYA when I was 16, and I was very shy. Once I had integrated into the TOYA atmosphere—where I played games, read books, shared ideas with the others, and started to speak in public—I became less shy and spoke more and without worries. They have become a family to me, and I grew up and learnt a lot about myself. Since then, I can say that my confidence has increased.

Thanks to Foundation TOYA, I had the opportunity to participate in the Global Girl Project (GGP) programme, which is about working with girls around the world on leadership. I think I was fortunate to become a member of the GGP family, where I could share ideas with other girls like me who don't speak the same

> "Despite our differences, we had the same reality and the same goal."

language that I do and don't have the same nationality as me. I felt that despite our differences, we had the same reality and the same goal, which was returning to our countries to support young people in our communities.

---

*Foundation TOYA is a non-profit organization, created for the supervision, capacity building and leadership of girls and women.

It was not easy for me to become a counsellor and help young girls around me with their choices because I was a very shy person. Before, I was afraid to speak so as not to make mistakes. I was afraid that people would laugh at me, but now, I am not scared anymore.

I remember the first time I had a project with young people in my community. The group was made up of young girls. Their parents always tell them what they are obliged to do. They need to know how to manage their houses, how to cook, and how to please their husbands. They do not have the opportunities to find careers or professions that they love. The boys, too, are being taught, but what they have to know is how to work hard to bring money to the house. This leads the girls to believe they do not need to have dreams or aspirations for themselves.

At that time, I doubted my capacities, but when I recognised all the challenges I had to face in Haitian society regarding gender equality, I was bold in my project. I want to provide these girls with the same chances I had and help them seize each opportunity. I believe that when you have a 100% trustworthy place where people don't consider which class of society you belong to, you have no problem developing your talents. This is because you are in contact with people who encourage you, not those who criticise you.

Having the opportunity to help young people in my community was something that I always wanted to do. It was, in fact, a dream come true. GGP gave me this opportunity. Now, I can say that I am one of the leaders in my community because the young girls believe in me and always need my advice. Now, I can achieve one of my grandest dreams, the dream of helping my fellow young girls. This means a lot to me, and I wanted to share it with you.

मेरो पशु परिवारलाई सम्मान गर्दै

Honouring My Animal Family

DEV MAYA
- from Nepal -

I was born in Rajghat, Nepal, a village with a population of 7,000 inhabitants. When I was still a child, we moved to Kathmandu, the capital city of Nepal. I think the main reason for us to move away was that Rajghat didn't have very good schools. It was a difficult choice. We had to leave my little sister behind in my Mamaghar (mother's hometown) while my mum, my dad, my brother, and I left for the big city.

We came from a small, tight community, and Kathmandu has more than two million inhabitants. We had no family, relatives or friends there, and everything was unfamiliar. We found a studio to rent, and my mum worked as a maid in strangers' homes. Her salary was just enough to pay the rent and our school expenses while my dad's salary was for groceries.

When I was around 5 years old, I was studying at a public school, and one day, after school, one of my friends asked if I would like to visit his place. I was really happy that a friend would invite me to his home, but when we got to Chabil, the area where my friend lived, he asked me to wait for him outside. I waited for four hours after which a shopkeeper came to ask me what I was doing there for so long. I explained that I was waiting for my friend. Since no one came to fetch me, the man asked for my parents' address and phone number so that he could contact them.

By then, my parents were very worried, and they had already gone to the school, searching for me. As soon as I got home, I ran to my mother and cried. They were very angry at me but also deeply worried that I had gone missing. From that day on, even though we had a hard time financially, my parents sent me to a private boarding school, which is much stricter and the children are watched more carefully. I never went back to the public school, and I never saw my friend again.

Now that I was going to a private boarding school, we didn't have enough money to cover all of our needs, so my father made a sacrifice by borrowing money from strangers. Luckily, after some time, my father cleared all of the loans, and my parents decided to bring my sister to our new home.

As a kid, like most kids do, I wanted to have good clothes but I never asked for them. My parents had to work so hard for all of us to eat and study that I felt it was unfair to ask for anything more. It was at times like this that I felt that money had great importance. My relatives never came visiting us because we were poor, but honestly, I did not feel poor. Even though we had very little, our family was happy.

"My parents had to work so hard for all of us to eat and study that I felt it was unfair to ask for anything more."

My whole family loves animals. When I was in class nine, I used to buy food for stray dogs from my pocket money. I felt that if my pocket money could help to feed the hungry, I would always be the first to help. I went to a school in my neighbourhood that took six minutes to walk there. At that time, I always took the same route home, and along the way, there were five or six stray dogs. I felt for them when they looked at me with big eyes. They were so cute that I gave them a cookie I had. My mum used to give me Rs. 20 a day for lunch money, and even though I liked saving money, I used most of it to buy more cookies so I could feed the dogs every time I passed by. The dogs would always recognise me, and every time I walked by, there would be even more of them. I loved them because I couldn't have dogs at home, but it felt like they were mine, and they brought me much happiness. This memory had an important role in my life later on.

"Even though we had very little, our family was happy."

In 2075 (Nepali calendar)*, I heard the news that I had been selected for the Global Girl Project (GGP). Although I felt fortunate, I was scared and not sure of what to do and how to conduct myself around foreign people. After some weeks, people from many countries came to Nepal along with the founder of GGP. I was very happy and excited.

We learnt many different things about project planning and public speaking, and we were taken to visit many interesting places. I did not feel confident about speaking English and had no leadership skills, but after talking to the other girls and doing workshops, I began to feel better about myself and started feeling the positive energy of leadership.

At the end of the training, we had to choose a project, so I chose to care for and give shelter to street dogs. I am really happy that I was able to set up my project and educate Nepali people about street dogs. This was something I had always wanted to do, but I didn't have the money to make it happen. Nepali people think of stray dogs as dirty, disgusting things. They mistreat them, kick them, and discriminate against people like me who enjoy helping them. Street dogs usually bark all night into the early hours of the morning, so people think they are trouble. I made it my task to teach people about dogs and how to treat and care for them. I even inspired other girls in my group to overcome their fears and welcome the warm love of dogs into their lives.

During the exchange programme, we went on a trek, and I had the chance to meet female mountain climber Pasang Lhamu Sherpa**. Thanks to that trek, I was inspired by Lhamu Sherpa and learnt to be more confident. What influenced me the most about her was that after a tough life of abuse, she left her husband at the age of 49 and went on to climb Mount Everest!

*Nepali Calendar uses lunar months and solar sidereal years. It is approximately 56 years and 8 months ahead of the English Gregorian Calendar.
**Pasang Lhamu Sherpa is a trekking guide in Nepal who summited Mt. Everest on May 16th, 2018.

I want to do the same. Five weeks went by so fast and soon enough, everyone went back home.

It did not stop there. We had to work on our projects in our communities, so I organised for me and nine friends to go to different animal shelters. Each week, we visited a local shelter and we walked, fed, and bathed the dogs. We also walked around the streets of our community and gave donated biscuits to street dogs.

"Everyone was so inspired by my leadership skills that I was hired by one of the organisations as a social worker."

Everyone was so inspired by my leadership skills that I was hired by one of the organisations as a social worker. While doing

my project, people took videos and photos of me as they felt inspired by my work.

In 2076, my friend and I had the chance to help new members of GGP as paid interns. We were very happy to help them and meet our new sisters. I always thank the founder for helping my sisters and me by mentoring and teaching us how to be leaders and build our confidence.

I am now 17 years old, and I find myself working toward the dream I had as a child while feeding the dogs cookies: providing shelter and food for stray dogs in Kathmandu.

A Garota que Venceu a Copa do Mundo

The Girl Who Won the World Cup

- from Brazil -

Hello. My name is Anny, and I was born in a small village in the interior of Sergipe, one of the smallest states in Brazil. I lived there for 13 years with my maternal grandparents. Life in Sergipe was not easy. We were very poor, and I didn't have as many toys as the other children, but nevertheless I was very content.

My mother left me with my grandparents because she went to Rio de Janeiro to look for a job. Where we lived, there were not many options for her. My grandparents eventually got sick and passed away. After this, I had to move to Rio de Janeiro and went to live with my mother, my stepfather and my brothers.

Living in Rio was very complicated from the beginning. I was not used to the hectic rhythm of life. Rio can be a very violent place,

too. While living in Sergipe, I was free. I could play outside all the time, sometimes until late in the evening. In Rio, even walking to the bakery is a risk. You could easily be robbed, attacked, or even shot dead.

I usually feel very nostalgic about my life in Sergipe, my freedom, my friends, my grandparents, and of course, the food. Rio is a gigantic city with millions of inhabitants, so far away from the little village where I grew up. My everyday reality now is full of trafficking, drugs, and dangerous people everywhere around me.

I had some disagreements with my stepfather, which ended badly, and he expelled me from our house. I first went to live with a boyfriend, then I moved in with an aunt and then I stayed with a cousin. I have now finally secured my own place, which I share with my dog. When I first left my mother and stepfather's house, I faced many challenges.

To start with, living away from home wasn't easy. I had no job, but I understood that I needed to grow up. I was no longer a little girl, and with the help of good people, I managed to continue my life and become who I am today—an independent woman.

In 2014, I was playing football outside with a group of friends, close to where I lived. A scout approached me and invited me to join the women's soccer team to represent Brazil in the Street Child World Cup* that was going to be held in Rio de Janeiro. It was such an incredible experience for me! I got the chance to meet children from different parts of the world, like Leonardo, a boy from Burundi, who had lost his parents in a war and had to live alone on the streets. He had no birth certificate and no passport. He told me he had to choose his own birthday. Even though his life was difficult, he had a wonderful smile.

---

*Ahead of the 2014 FIFA World Cup in Brazil, the Street Child World Cup in association with Save the Children, united 230 street-connected children representing 19 countries to play in their own international football tournament, festival of arts and Congress for their rights.

What made this experience even more memorable is that we beat the Philippines' team in an intense game to become the winners of the championship. After the World Cup, my team coach had to return to Holland, where he was from. Because I was the team captain, I accepted the responsibility to continue working in the project that was called Favela Street Girls*.

"I had never been on a plane before and I didn't know how to speak English."

This is the reason why, in 2015, I was invited to go to the United States to be part of GGP. It was my first trip out of the country, and it was a unique opportunity I did not want to miss. I was so nervous on that first trip. I had never been on a plane before, and I didn't know how to speak English, yet I was going to a country that spoke that language. I remember I kept asking God for everything to go well.

When I arrived in Los Angeles, the airline lost my luggage. Losing my luggage was frustrating, and I didn't know what to do to get it back. I spoke with an airport security guard who luckily spoke Spanish, and we could follow each other a little bit because it is very similar to Portuguese, and she helped me find the suitcase. I was frightened, but in the end, everything went well, and I lived for two months with wonderful people.

One of the most memorable moments was participating in several workshops with the founder of GGP. I even did capoeira. How strange it was for a Brazilian woman to practice it for the first time in the USA (Brazil is the land of capoeira)! After being a part of this project, many other doors opened. I spent two months in England studying English, I went to Germany for a youth

*Favela Street is founded on the conviction that street football applied to socially challenging environments can help youngsters overcome the difficulties of their situation and reach their full potential.

leadership programme, and I went to Dallas for Michael Johnson Positive Track. Afterwards, I got to visit Russia for the Street Child World Cup.

My present life is still in Rio, where I work on the Street Child United - Caracol Family Social Project* in the Penha community, one of the most dangerous areas in Brazil. I coach football and offer life skills to children and young people between ages 5-18. I feel proud of the woman I am becoming, more mature, more knowledgeable and responsible, supporting other children as I was supported. I love every child I work with as if they were my own.

"I feel proud of the woman I am becoming, more mature, more knowledgeable and responsible."

I know how difficult it is to live in a Rio community where there is excessive street violence, a lack of basic sanitation and drugs are common currency. My job is to help these kids while growing up and to support them so that they will become good adults with great jobs. Also, I'm studying physical education. This was certainly one of my childhood dreams, in case the plans to be a soccer player didn't work out! I'm happy to be in college and I'm happy to have used every opportunity offered to me. I am happy for all the knowledge I've acquired along the way. I am very grateful for all the people who have helped me so far. My plan now is to get to know projects like mine in other parts of the world and help them in any way I can.

*Familia Caracol is an initiative of NGO Street Child United Brazil, where boys and girls can play on their streets without any judgement, violence, guns or drugs.

Guhitamo Ubuzima

Life's Choices

LUCY
- from Cameroon -

One lesson I'll never forget was when my mom told me about never giving up and always striving to reach my goals.

My name is Lucy, and I was born in a little village in the northwest region of Cameroon. I have two younger siblings and two older siblings. I grew up in a very large family with a lot of cousins and nephews. Growing up, I was always ambitious, and I have always tried to be the best in everything I do. I never gave up on my dreams, although I was not from a privileged family.

Studying in school was very hard and stressful as my parents could not afford to buy all of my textbooks and school materials.

Sometimes, I was sent home from school because of incomplete fees, and other times I would be sent out of class because I did not have some of the books required. Even though all this was happening, I did not stop working hard. What kept me going and made me stronger was my positive spirit and the advice I received from my parents.

After I took the national exams, I was supposed to start high school. At that time, political instability in Cameroon caused all of the schools to close, and my siblings and I had to stay home for two years without any education. Kids seen going to school were shot dead, and schools were burnt down. During this time, I assisted my mom with a small business she was running.

In January 2018, my aunt, who lived in Rwanda, suggested to my mom that I could go and stay with her. She offered to assist with my education, and I could help her at home and take care of her kids. This was a great opportunity for me to continue my education, and I remain forever grateful to my aunt for what she did for my family and me.

I moved immediately to Rwanda and started my education at White Dove Global Prep*. I loved the school because it was an all-girls school, and everyone seemed nice and caring. In my second year of studying in Rwanda, my teacher told me about the five-week Global Girl Project (GGP) leadership opportunity which would take place in Nepal. I got very excited about this opportunity, as I imagined meeting new people with different backgrounds and cultures. I applied immediately to be able to participate in this leadership training and luckily, I was chosen.

My classmate and I travelled to Nepal together. We were a bit tense as we had never travelled alone before, but we received a lot of encouragement from our parents, teachers, friends, and the director of GGP.

*White Dove Global Prep is a primary, O & A Level E- STEAM-focused Christian school offering college prep academics for all levels.

On our arrival in Nepal, we had a warm welcome at the airport, and we were taken to where we would live while we were there. I got to meet different people who were very welcoming and loving. They made me feel like I was home and a part of their family.

"I got to understand people and cultures with different ideologies than mine."

I got to understand people and cultures with different ideologies than mine. This helped me to learn and understand that no matter who you are or where you are, you can communicate and interact with others as long as you respect their backgrounds and beliefs.

I visited many tourist sites and got to see amazing architecture and buildings. One of my favourite experiences was when we went hiking. I learnt that no matter how difficult or impossible a task can be, if you put in your best effort and always think positively, it can be achieved!

My confidence in public speaking increased as I got out of my shy zone and took the initiative to talk and socialise more with different people.

The director of GGP was a role model to me, as I admired her confidence and how she always encouraged me at times when I was in difficult situations. Also, I liked how she

"I learnt that no matter how difficult or impossible a task can be, if you put in your best effort and always think positively, it can be achieved!"

strives to impact the lives of many girls around the world to make them better leaders.

My GGP experience in Nepal was a lot of fun. I recall many people coming up to me, wanting to touch my hair or asking me if I can take a photo with them. A lot of people stared at me in surprise as I walked on the streets, mostly because I was black. My experience in Nepal was one of the most memorable moments of my life.

I'm very happy today, back in Rwanda. I run my own project, supporting young teenage girls and teaching them about the effects of early pregnancy on their lives and education. My leadership and public speaking skills are well-established, and I can now talk to different individuals and large groups of people without being afraid or nervous as I was before.

Learning to be a good leader, being confident and believing in yourself, are very important in society today. Not only does it have a positive impact on your personal life, but you get the chance to influence and encourage others with your actions. Changing the world requires changing one person at a time.

عورت کی طاقت

Strength of a Woman

- from Pakistan -

I belong to a society where women are often oppressed, and their decisions are imposed on them. I have heard members of my community say that girls will only ever get married and perform basic household duties; therefore, study is wasted on them. It becomes very difficult for women to feel that they deserve better choices.

This should not happen to women. I have the courage to make changes. I believe that girls should have control over their lives and decisions so they can also be successful people. I believe that girls do not need the support of their families to achieve success, especially when their families believe they are not capable. I want to show my community that there are other possible ways to look at this issue. I believe that a successful man can provide for a good home but I also believe that a successful woman can make all of society successful.

In my community, the belief that girls should not get a higher education is very prominent. Even my parents were urged to ask me to drop out of school after I had passed my exams, but my parents, who are well educated, knew the importance of a high-school education. My father is a politician, and my mum is a health worker, and they spoke openly to the people in my community about the fact that girls have the same right to education as boys.

When I was in the eleventh grade, my father had a sudden stroke, and his condition was very bad. The doctors said that it would be very difficult for him to recover.

At that time, my exams were going on. I could not perform well and I failed on the first try. It was a very difficult time for me. When I saw my father so sick, I cried and felt weak. I didn't know what to do. It was the first time I saw my father get emotional and cry. The stroke caused him to lose his memory.

After he recovered, I was readmitted to school at the beginning of 2019. It was at this time that my cousin's sister informed us about the Seeds of Hope Foundation*. My auntie had already worked with the foundation and knew a lot about it. She told my parents that the foundation was looking for two Pakistani girls to join a project run by Global Girl Project (GGP) in Nepal. The procedure to enrol took a long time for a few reasons.

My family wanted me to stay home to take care of my father. It was also unusual for young girls from Pakistan to travel outside the country, especially without their parents, but once a chaperone was found, my parents agreed to let me be a part of this project.

*Seeds of Hope Foundation is an International human rights, advocacy, and development organization working with the marginalized communities in Pakistan.

"It was unusual for young girls from Pakistan to travel outside the country."

Before we left for Nepal, the director of GGP explained the characteristics of the project to us through online meetings. I felt awkward at first because I had never met anyone online before, and I had never had to speak in English so much, but what I remember most clearly was that the real purpose of the project was to teach girls leadership skills.

It was the first time I had been to an airport and travelled by plane. Nepal and Pakistan are quite different in terms of dress code, language, and culture. There were many other girls who came from other countries besides Pakistan. At first, I thought it was weird because the girls seemed different to me. They spoke different languages and followed different religions, but over time, we became very good friends. I saw many temples and different religious rituals, some from religions I had never seen before, as a part of our sightseeing activities. This left a strong impact on my understanding, especially about Buddhism.

Most of the time, we were busy participating in workshops where we developed our projects. As GGP participants, we had to choose our own projects and lead them to completion ourselves. GGP taught me a lot, and I am not like I was before. Today, I am so confident, and I am stronger than I thought I could be.

"It was the first time I had been to an airport and travelled by plane."

My project name was "Strength of Women", and it was about teaching women handicrafts and business skills. I chose this project because my goal was to help women change themselves.

I wanted to inspire them to have confidence in themselves by teaching them skills they could use to earn their own money and be more independent. Even though my project was small, everyone was excited to learn something new.

Although my project is finished now, that doesn't mean that I have forgotten the women who took part. Whenever they have problems, they come to talk to me. They consulted with me on how to deal with the coronavirus spreading all over the world and about the shortage of food, but we could not find immediate solutions, so I decided to go out to get food for those who were in need.

"Today I am so confident, I am stronger than I thought I could be."

I shared my problems with the director of GGP, and she gave me the idea to go around, asking people who are financially comfortable for help. At the time, my mum said that the extra food we had was for us. I thought that if I wanted to change things in my community, then I had to start at home, and I tried to convince my mum that it was the right thing to do. She said that the idea was good, but it was not enough to make her change her mind. It took time and a lot of explaining about how we had too much extra food while there were people in our area who had none.

Thankfully, she finally agreed to help me talk to those who were financially better off to ask for help. I got together with a group of friends, and we went knocking door-to-door, collecting food and making packages that we delivered to those who needed them most. At that time, I felt like a leader. I learnt that if you have courage and determination, everything seems to be easier for you. My name is Jiya. I live in Pakistan, I am 18 years old, and one day, I will buy myself a really nice motorcycle. Those who have met me know why. 🌍

यसको कभर द्वारा पुस्तक न्याय नगर्नुहोस्

Don't Judge a Book by its Cover

SMRITI
- from Nepal -

The only wish I ever had was to study. At the age of five, I left my village and went to stay and work with my aunt. I had to work very hard to receive an education but being able to learn is the most important thing in my life.

I come from a very poor family of farmers. We are a big family, so we all have to work a lot to sustain our lives here. To survive, we had to give up all other interests and dreams. We didn't have much to eat, and I never thought about pursuing anything outside the norm.

I had to study at a government school while my brother could study in a boarding school. I think I was of little importance to my parents, as I am a girl, but actually, I am very happy that God made me a girl. Some might say that physically, I am weak compared to boys, but mentally, I am strong, and a strong mindset is better than physical fitness.

From the age of six, apart from my duties at home, I used to work for other households, doing tasks such as cleaning, washing dishes, and babysitting. My school fee was Rs. 250 per term, and even though I always saved money from my tips, I usually did not have the money to pay, and I cried a lot. My friends at school used to look down on me because I was poor, and I had to work away from home. Since then, I always had the strong

feeling that we should never discriminate against poor people, and I always remembered the importance of saving money. Studying was very hard, but I always encouraged myself while doing my studies. I knew that I could be whatever I wanted to be. No one is 100% perfect, and to achieve the dreams we dream, we have to work really hard.

My name is Smriti. I was born in Rawa Village in the Kotang District, Nepal. Rawa Village is a lot more undeveloped than other villages, and most of the people are uneducated. Although there are many resources, the people don't have the means to take advantage of them. Most people are involved in farming and animal husbandry, but they don't know how to use modern technology because of their lack of education. Most adults still believe in the old traditions and differentiate the capacities of boys and girls.

To me, it is very important to change my village. Most teenage girls are unable to acquire an education here, so they migrate to bigger cities, but if there were proper health, education, and communication facilities, they would probably stay in their homes with their parents and they would help develop their own village.

Most of the poor people here are co-operative, generous, and kind. They never cheat or betray other people as they are honest and sincere when it comes to their duties and responsibilities. I believe that nature and gods never discriminate between people. It's us, the human beings, who make these distinctions. All people are different and have talents in them since birth. We should be happy and satisfied with what we are. I believe that if I am loyal and honest, then I will never be left out. I see the good side of being poor because the situation has made me an understanding, loyal, and honest person. If I weren't in this situation, I might not be the person I am today, and I want to encourage other girls by writing my story.

Caste discrimination is the main problem in my village. Rich people do not allow poor people to enter their homes. Poor people never have opportunities to develop or grow. I was given an opportunity, and Global Girl Project (GGP) taught me confidence and leadership skills. I never believed in myself because I was poor, but the workshops gave me self-confidence.

"I knew that I could be whatever I wanted to be. No one is 100% perfect, and to achieve the dreams we dream, we have to work really hard."

When I returned to Rawa Village after taking part in GGP, I wrote a play related to caste discrimination, and many teenage girls helped me with the performance. I performed it in my village, and through watching my play, many people changed their thoughts, and I saw some change in my village! People started to think positively and treated every person equally. The play included different social problems and was related to my personal life, like how my parents discriminated against me because I was a girl, and how some rich people from private schools treated me differently because I wore old clothes. It was hard for me because I was alone while conducting this programme, but later, many teenage girls gave me their support and showed me their love.

The experience has given me strength, and I will study so I can encourage teenage girls in my village to find their own strength. I will educate poor people by running programmes against discrimination between girls and boys. I want others to learn how to be mentally strong and not judge people by their possessions or social status. I feel proud of myself because I have been able to achieve a part of this.

I say, "Don't judge a book by its cover."

Nya Hala Levu Jai

My First Life Journey

AISATA
- from Sierra Leone -

This is my life story, and it goes like this:

I grew up in a small community called Bumpe Ngao Chiefdom in Sierra Leone, West Africa. Growing up as a girl was not easy. Being a girl in my community means that as early as the age of 12, it is possible to get married and get pregnant, both inside and outside of marriage. It happens all the time, and here, the effects of early pregnancies are very dangerous. They can include early death, poor parental care, dropping out of school, and earning a bad reputation within the community. I always felt that this wouldn't be my future and that I was going to make better decisions.

My name is Aisata, and I am 19 years of age. I am black in complexion, Mende by tribe, Christian by religion, and Sierra Leonean by nationality. I live with my mother, and I have two brothers and one sister. My mother is a trader, and my father is a teacher. They separated during the rebel war in 2000. My father lives in a remote village where he works as a volunteer teacher. There was no school in this region until he decided to build a mud-block house to be used as one. He wants to help children access education in that part of the country to become good leaders in the future.

At the age of seven, I began my formal education at a school in Bumpe Ngao. After a while, I moved to Freetown, the capital city of Sierra Leone. I was there for 12 years. I went to live with my auntie, my mother's eldest sister. She was never really nice to me, and she did not treat me like her sister's daughter, like family. I was more like a fellow villager.

While her children attended good and expensive private schools, I was sent to a modest public school. My mum used to visit once a year, and whenever my auntie thought my mum was about to pay me a visit, she would call me aside and threaten me. If my mother were to ask anything about her and how she was taking care of me, I should say nothing bad about her, and I should not complain. I was only to say good things, anytime, to any question. I always felt bad about myself after this. Before my mother left the city, she would always remind me that I promised her I would become a leader, and as a good leader, I was expected to understand all of life's troubles.

After some years of living this way, I made up my mind to leave my auntie's house. I convinced her that, after I had moved up into grade eight, it would be an excellent idea if I moved back to my village. She said she had expected that, and she was even happy that I would return home. She thought that me going back to the village meant that I would drop out of school, get married, and bear children, like so many other girls there. However, I resumed my education in Bumpe Ngao, where people respected me and admired my determination. I used to tell my friends and family about the troubles and suffering I went through while in Freetown.

As a young child, I discovered beauty in everything. I dreamt about sitting on a plane and travelling to another country, but I was discouraged by my parents who told me that we were too poor and therefore I should not keep my hopes up. No one from their families had ever been to another country, not even Liberia, which is a neighbouring country, but I was about to prove them wrong.

"I dreamt about sitting on a plane and travelling to another country."

When I was about to go into grade ten, I was called for an interview with a Canadian woman from the organisation Global Girl Project (GGP). They had selected more than five students from our class who were interviewed by her, and luckily, I was the one selected to participate in their international exchange programme. I was really happy, and my parents were happy for me, that I was finally able to travel to a distant country: Nepal. My mother called my auntie and told her the whole story, and my auntie was ashamed of herself and the way she had treated me.

Once I had reached Nepal, everything about my life changed. I made many new friends, and I stayed with locals who offered me traditional Nepali homemade food, which is similar to Indian food. One thing I learnt in Nepal was that food certainly tells you a great deal about a culture and its people, and this is why trying out the new dishes was always exciting for me. Nepali meals consist of rice along with a variety of side dishes, including dhal, vegetables, salads, and pickles. Nepali food was a little bit on the plain side for my taste buds, but that is only because of my upbringing with a lot of spicy foods. Interesting dishes I tasted included rice, ripe mangoes, and rose corn, which were fantastic.

Although before, I thought I would be capable of keeping the promise to my mum to be a great leader, I was insecure, and I lacked self-confidence. In Nepal, I discovered new things about myself, and the way I thought about myself changed. Being able to connect with people was not sufficient for me to be successful—I needed to be strong, courageous, hardworking, kind, and have discipline. I listened and paid attention to all that I was taught, and when I returned home, I was able to create the change I had dreamt of for so long. I learnt that a leader is someone who can see how things can be improved and rallies people to move toward a better future. Knowing what it means to be a leader continues to benefit me in many different ways.

> "Knowing what it means to be a leader continues to benefit me in many different ways."

On my return to Sierra Leone, I led a project called "Let Marriage Wait". Early marriage is a marriage between two people in which one or both parties are younger than 18 years of age. Parents often feel that young girls are an economic burden, and they wish to marry them off before they become financial liabilities.

When I was 11 years old, I realised that my country was suffering from so much injustice that I made up my mind to become a lawyer so I could help my country stand for the truth. My parents told me that we were too poor, but I told them, "That is the same thing you said to me when I dreamt of travelling to distant countries, and I made that dream come true." I promise I will make this one happen, too. 🌍

COMMUNITY ACTION PROJECTS

All GGP scholars work on a community project they are required to design and implement as a part of their graduation from the programme. In running their projects, not only do our scholars learn how to lead in a hands-on way, but they also become attainable role models for other young people in their communities. Through her project, each scholar shows those around her that there are many different ways to be a girl. Listed below are the projects the authors in this book have mentioned in their stories that were run in their local cities, towns, and remote villages.

SHREE - INDIA

Shree partnered with local orphanages to run sessions with their children and teach them how to use dance as a way to express themselves and work through their issues. This programme was run within the local red-light district in Mumbai, India. Shree is a young woman who is full of energy and loves to dance to all types of music, and she has used dancing as a way to work through some of her life's traumas. Shree knew the children living in local orphanages were not being taught how to express their challenges and pain in this way, and she wanted to teach them how to express themselves through dance. The children Shree worked with expressed a great deal of joy in her sessions and were grateful for their time with her as their local role model. Since the GGP leadership training programme ended, Shree shared that she realised she has to make herself stronger, and she needs to accept her past to create a better future. Her journey since being a GGP participant has changed because she can now proudly say that she is a good leader, and even though it is difficult to lead, she has become a leader for both herself and her community.

ASHLEYCKA - HAITI

Ashleycka's project focused on the issue of gender inequality in her home community of Port-au-Prince, Haiti. She knew that very few conversations were being had with the children in her community about how gender inequality affects their lives, so she facilitated weekly sessions with boys and girls of primary school age that included guest speakers as well as sessions run by her. As her sessions progressed, Ashleycka could see that the participants' points of view were changing dramatically, and they felt they had a safe space to express their desire for community change around this issue. Working on this project confirmed Ashleycka's love of working with children and clarified her goal of becoming a paediatrician.

DEV MAYA - NEPAL

Dev Maya's passion for street dogs was evident from the moment she started our programme. The grin on her face every time she passed one in the streets was enough to make everyone smile. In Nepal, there are many dogs living wild on the streets. They are often sick and malnourished, and the locals feel they are a nuisance because they enter stores and people's houses, and they bark all night, keeping up the neighbours. Dev Maya decided that she wanted to change her community members' opinions towards street dogs and ensure they were better cared for. Dev Maya was able to gather a large group of community members of all ages who had previously had a distaste for street dogs, and they worked together for more than three months to change the plight of the local strays. Together with this group, Dev Maya volunteered at local animal shelters, bathing, feeding, and walking their dogs. Additionally, she was able to get local restaurants to donate expiring food that the group fed to local street dogs on their weekly walks around the community. Dev Maya continues her work to this day.

ANNY - BRAZIL

As our first exchange student, Anny was brave enough to choose to go through our brand-new programme and return back home to Brazil to work on her project. Initially, Anny chose to focus on her education and completing school. Nevertheless, as soon as she was able, she continued to work with Favela Street Girls to give back to so many girls what she had received herself, the knowledge that with support and strength they could become leaders. To this day, Anny continues to run a football and life skills programme for young people in the Penha community in Rio de Janeiro. Her passion for giving young girls the opportunity to express themselves through sport and to have a safe place to exist is what drives her forward every day. Anny knew that without a positive place to spend their time and energy, girls in the Penha community could get into a lot of trouble. Anny saw that many girls had become involved in drugs and gangs and were often pregnant at an early age. Through her own experiences, Anny was able to connect with the girls who attended her programming to help them see a different way forward for themselves as girls, and eventually, as young women. Anny's travel experience with GGP was the first of many, as she continued to travel with the Street Child World Cup, sharing her story and her strength with many others around the globe!

LUCY - CAMEROON

Lucy wanted to address the very real issue of teenage pregnancy that exists within Rwanda. She felt that many of her peers had become pregnant due to a lack of education about how to protect themselves during sex and the lack of understanding of how becoming a young mother could change their lives. Lucy started her project by reaching out to various schools in the Kigali area, asking if she could run workshops with their students. It took a lot of perseverance, but Lucy was able to convince a number of schools to work with her in partnership toward her goal of reducing the rate of teenage pregnancy in Rwanda. Due to the coronavirus pandemic, at the time of writing this book, Lucy has had to put her project on hold until the restrictions of lockdown have ceased.

JIYA - PAKISTAN

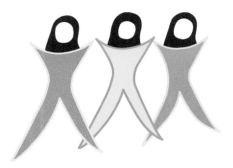

Strength of Women

Jiya was focused on the development of her project from the beginning of the exchange programme. She felt very strongly about the challenges faced by some women in her home country of Pakistan around being viewed as equal to men. Jiya wanted to offer women in her community the opportunity to learn a trade that would help them become more independent and earn money separately from their husbands, so she found women who volunteered in her community and offered to run handicraft-making workshops to a group of around 20 women. Another volunteer ran business development workshops for women. Jiya reported that the majority of the women participating felt a stronger sense of independence and greater confidence about their ability to take care of themselves. She also reported that about half of the women continued on to start up their own small handicraft businesses. At the host school in Nepal, you could often find Jiya sitting on one of the many motorcycles parked in the yard. She dreams of riding a motorcycle one day, which is something that is not expected of her as a young woman living in Pakistan.

SMRITI - NEPAL

Caste discrimination is a significant issue for many communities in Nepal, especially within more remote villages. Smriti is from a small village close to Mt. Everest and has experienced this issue first-hand. She wanted to develop a project to engage her peers in educating their community about the problems caused by caste discrimination. To achieve this, Smriti did something frowned upon within her community: she spoke with authority to her elders. Smriti did this with confidence because she knew that she needed the support of the chairman of her village and the other village elders to get her project up and running. After receiving their support, Smriti did a lot of outreach within her peer group and recruited a number of young people from different castes to come together to create a play about caste discrimination. The group also made flyers with slogans about caste equality and posted them around the village. After much preparation, Smriti and her cast performed their play in front of large crowds in their village square. Smriti reported that the villagers were very enthusiastic about their storytelling and started to see aspects of this issue in a different light.

AISATA - SIERRA LEONE

Aisata is a determined and focused young woman who feels that girls shouldn't let anything get in their way when accessing a good education. Aisata felt that in her village in Sierra Leone, many teenage girls were getting married at 13 or 14 years of age and that the consequences of this were life-changing. These girls ultimately got pregnant and left school, so Aisata decided to create a project to work with young boys and girls, as well as their parents, to educate them about the importance of waiting until adulthood to be married. Aisata gained the support and trust of her village chief to run weekly sessions with groups of community members where experts in the field would come to speak with them about different options surrounding marriage. Aisata had 60 to 80 community members attending her sessions on a weekly basis. They were so successful she was asked by representatives of neighbouring communities to speak there as well. What is so important about this project is that Aisata opened up the lines of communication in her village and gave people, young and old alike, a space to discuss this important issue.

ABOUT GLOBAL GIRL PROJECT
AND OUR LEADERSHIP

Global Girl Project (GGP) is a unique initiative dedicated to mobilising socially-minded young women, who live in poverty within developing countries, to become leaders. Our exchange and online programmes are designed to enrich skills-sets, generate support, and provide knowledge for these young leaders to implement unique initiatives that support their home communities. In doing so we access the untapped potential that exists within women and girls, 51% of the world's population, by creating transformative experiences that mobilise and motivate girls to lead impactful community change.

The founding director of GGP is Julia Lynch. Over the past 20 years, Julia has worked as a Community Social Worker and Therapist in Canada, Great Britain, and the United States, and on a volunteer basis in both Tanzania and Jamaica providing community and health services to local at-risk communities. She is the innovator and developer of all our programming. Julia works in partnership with NGOs and schools globally to implement and run leadership programmes and initiatives for girls. She not only works directly with our scholars, both online and in Nepal, but also runs the day-to-day operations of GGP from the United Kingdom. A role model to our own scholars, Julia is also a force for positive change further afield, speaking to businesses and organizations globally about how to be a change-maker in one's own life, world and work.

Global
Girl
Project

www.globalgirlproject.org

Conscious Dreams
PUBLISHING

Be the author of your own destiny

Find out about our authors, events, services
and how you too can get your book journey started.

f Conscious Dreams Publishing

🐦 @DreamsConscious

📷 @consciousdreamspublishing

in Daniella Blechner

www www.consciousdreamspublishing.com

✉ info@consciousdreamspublishing.com

Let's connect

MORE THAN ONE VOICE

Lightning Source UK Ltd.
Milton Keynes UK
UKHW051335060322
399624UK00002B/6